Lyme Regis to Poole Harbour

Part of the England Coast Path

Text: *Dennis Kelsall*
Series editor: *Tony Bowerman*
Photographs: *Dennis Kelsall, Tony Bowerman, Adobe Stock, Dreamstime, Shutterstock*

Design: *Carl Rogers*

Northern
Eye

Northern Eye Books

ISBN 978-1-908632-69-2

A CIP catalogue record for this book is available from the British Library.

www.northerneyebooks.co.uk

Cover: *Old Harry Rocks (walk 10)*

Important Advice: The routes described in this book are undertaken at the reader's own risk. Walkers should take into account their level of fitness, wear suitable footwear and clothing, and carry food and water. It is also advisable to take the relevant OS map with you in case you get lost and leave the area covered by our maps.

Whilst every care has been taken to ensure the accuracy of the route directions, the publishers cannot accept responsibility for errors or omissions, or for changes in the details given. Nor can the publisher and copyright owners accept responsibility for any consequences arising from the use of this book.

If you find any inaccuracies in either the text or maps, please either write to us or email us at the addresses below. Thank you.

First published in 2018 by:

Northern Eye Books Limited

Northern Eye Books, Tattenhall, Cheshire CH3 9PX
Email: tony@northerneyebooks.com

For sales enquiries, please call: 01928 723 744

www.englandcoastpath.co.uk
www.northerneyebooks.co.uk
www.top10walks.co.uk

Twitter: @Northerneyeboo

Contents

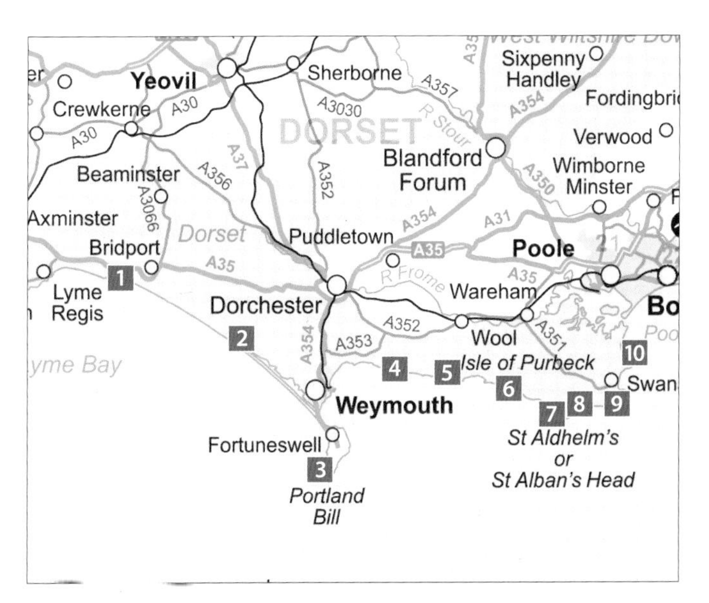

Yeovil
Sherborne
Sixpenny Handley
Fordingbri
Crewkerne
A30
A3030
A357
A354
DORSET
R Stour
Verwood
Blandford Forum
Wimborne Minster
Beaminster
A356
A37
A352
A350
A3066
Axminster
Dorset
Puddletown
A354
A31
Bridport
A35
Poole
Lyme Regis
R Frome
Wareham
Dorchester
A352
Wool
A351
Bo
yme Bay
A354
A353
Isle of Purbeck
Swan
Weymouth
Fortuneswell
St Aldhelm's or St Alban's Head
Portland Bill
1
2
3
4
5
6
7
8
9
10

South West Coast Path

Running for 650 miles from Minehead in Somerset, around the tip of Land's End and back to South Haven Point at the mouth of Poole Harbour in Dorset, the South West Coast Path is Britain's longest National Trail. Bordered by the Bristol and English channels and looking out to the open Atlantic, it encompasses some of England's most spectacular and wildest coastline, where the diversity of plant, animal and insect life can be stunning. The seas, coves and surrounding hinterland has been a dramatic setting for a gloriously rich history, which has inspired countless tales of romance, drama and intrigue.

This series of Top Ten Walks explores highlights along the way; showcasing its natural beauty, wildlife and heritage and provoking imagination. Who knows, you may be inspired to come back to tackle the complete trail.

Durdle Door is a natural limestone arch on the Jurassic Coast near Lulworth, Dorset

Dorset's '**Jurassic Coast**'

A UNESCO World Heritage Site, the southwest Jurassic Coast stretches almost 100 miles from Studland in Dorset to Lyme Regis in Devon. Layered in the geology and fossils of its cliffs is an almost unbroken record of 185 million years of the earth's history. During that time, continental drift and climate change have completely altered the earth's landscape, while periodic extinctions have wiped out whole species and allowed new life forms to flourish. Gradual erosion is revealing secrets from that past, helping piece together the fascinating story of our world.

> "World Heritage Site [status] is an extremely prestigious but well-earned distinction for the Jurassic Coast."
>
> Sir David Attenborough, OM CH FRS

Top 10 Walks: Dorset's Jurassic Coast

THE DORSET COAST IS PERHAPS THE MOST VARIED of the whole south western peninsula, encompassing glorious beaches, towering cliffs, detached stacks, long shingle banks and picturesque coves and inlets. The handiwork of man both past and present is there too, in settlement, quarrying and even oil extraction. But there is little to detract from the coast's overall beauty — and the coast's huge range of habitats is reflected in the sheer abundance of flowers and wildlife you'll experience along the way.

Durdle Door &
Lulworth Cove
page 30
Kimmeridge
Ledges
page 36
St Aldhelm's Head
page 42
Dancing Ledge
page 48

Durlston Head
page 54
Old Harry Rocks
page 58

A vivid storm-light illuminates the cliffs near Golden Cap

Golden Cap

Spectacular views, beaches and a 'lost' medieval village on a ramble over the highest point on Britain's southern coastline

What to expect:
A longer walk with several sustained, steep ascents, but on good paths and tracks throughout

Distance/time: 12 kilometres/ 7½ miles. Allow 4½ to 5 hours

Start: Stonebarrow Hill car park (NT - pay and display)

Grid refs: SY 383 933

Map: Ordnance Survey Explorer OL15: Purbeck & South Dorset

After the walk: Light refreshment at National Trust shop at start OR The Anchor Inn, Seatown DT6 6JU | 01297 489215 | www.theanchorinnseatown.co.uk

Walk outline

Leaving the open heath and woodland of Stonebarrow Hill, the route joins an undulating section of the coast path before tackling the steep ascent to the top of Golden Cap. The path then steadily loses height to Seatown, where an inviting inn sits above the beach. The rising return follows an old lane to skirt the plantation of Langdon Hill before descending a quiet stream valley to the ancient hamlet of St Gabriel's. The last leg climbs to Upcot and on around the slope of Chardown Hill before concluding in a final easy ascent back to Stonebarrow.

Coast Path sign

Golden Cap

At 191 metres high, Golden Cap is the highest point along the whole of Britain's southern coast, and a prominent landmark from Portland Bill all the way to Start Point in Devon, almost 50 miles away. Its name derives from the honey-coloured layer of sandstone capping its summit, a layer of rock laid down as the Jurassic period came to an end. The buttressing cliffs either side are steadily collapsing into the sea and the disintegrating boulders on the beach below have revealed many fossils.

Golden samphire

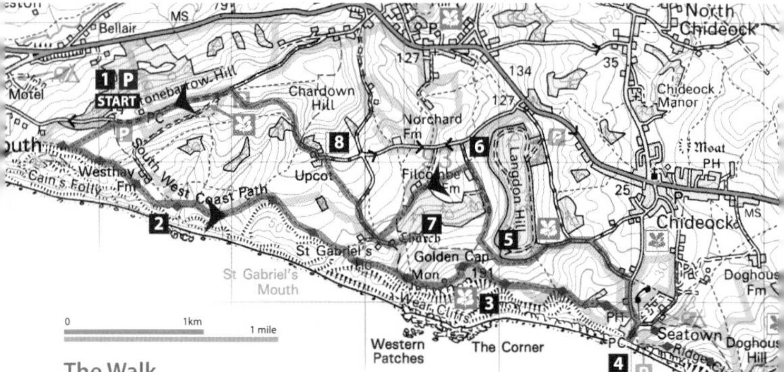

The Walk

1. Beginning from the **National Trust shop**, head back down the track to the bottom of the parking area. Branch off left at the edge of the **heath**, following a marked footpath to 'the coast'. At the end, go left again along the **coast path** above **Cain's Folly**, part of a massive ongoing cliffslip that runs all the way to Seatown. Fingerposts mark the route, which keeps well back from the crumbling edge, and steadily falls behind **Westhay Farm** to a **bridge** spanning a stream in a wooded gully.

2. Climb away over a grassy rise, dropping once more to cross another tree-girt gully, **Ridge Water**. The way rises again, passing a three-way fingerpost and eventually leading to a kissing gate on the right. Beyond, another gentle descent falls to a third stream above **St Gabriel's Mouth**. A steep, stepped path then begins the ascent to **Golden Cap**, ultimately zigzagging through bracken to ease the final pull. Carry on past a **a small stone monument** to a trig column.

The memorial commemorates Randal McDonnell, 8th Earl of Antrim, who as Chairman of the National Trust in 1965 oversaw the founding of Enterprise Neptune. Since then, some 580 miles of coast has been acquired, bringing the total now protected by the Trust to 775 miles.

3. A stepped path drops left to a gate, through which 'Seatown' is signed to the right. Continue down the hillside, the way obviously signed, eventually

Seatown seafood: *The Anchor Inn serves award-winning seafood and other dishes*

crossing the middle of a field to follow an enclosed path out to a lane. Turn right to the **beach** and **The Anchor Inn**.

Just about everywhere along Dorset's Jurassic Coast, erosion and landslip are revealing the fossils of long extinct animals and plants, which have been preserved within the rocks, shales and mud of the cliffs. Washed out by the surging waves, they can most easily be found by searching the foreshore on a falling tide, either scattered amongst the pebbles and shingle of the beach or revealed in the crumbling mudstone underfoot. Commonly found are ammonites, an ancient spiral-shelled mollusc, which looked something like the present day nautilus, and belemnites, a squid-like animal whose hard parts are usually preserved as a bullet shaped stone. Complete finds of larger creatures such as the ichthyosaur are rare, but small teeth and vertebrae are plentiful.

4. Head back up the lane for 500 metres to find a track leaving on the left past **Seahill House** towards **Langdon Woods**. Stick with the main banked

Sea view: *Looking west towards Charmouth from the lofty summit of Golden Cap*

track past two junctions and then take a path off left, eventually reaching a junction of paths by a gate.

5. Go through the gate into a meadow and strike out half-right to a five-bar gate that then comes into view. Continue across the next field below the wooded slopes of **Langdon Hill** to another gate. An enclosed path leads on beside the field edge, crossing a stile and soon joining a track past **Filcombe Farm**.

6. Immediately beyond the buildings, leave through a gate on the left towards **St Gabriel's**. Head downfield beside the hedge, passing through a gate at the bottom corner. Take the path ahead at the perimeter of **St Gabriel's Wood**, continuing through successive gates and crossing a **bridge** before eventually meeting a track. Walk left, through a gate to a junction by a thatched manor house, **Elm Cottage** and go left again up to the **ruined church of St Gabriel's**.

7. Retrace your steps past Elm Cottage and down the track, carrying on through a dip and up to a sharp right-hand bend. Leave just after over a stile on the left.

Head up the field edge, exiting at the top past **stock pens** onto an old lane.

8. Go left and then swing right through **Upcot Farm**, continuing up the hill beyond. Over the crest, pass through a gate and keep ahead towards **Stonebarrow Hill**. The way winds up across bracken heath, ultimately leading through a gate for the final pull to the top of Stonebarrow. **The National Trust shop** lies to the left down the main track, to complete the walk. ♦

Stanton St Gabriel

Shipwrecked in a stormy sea, Bertram and his bride prayed to St Gabriel, promising to build a chapel if they reached land. Tragically, his wife died as he eventually carried her ashore, but Bertram kept his promise. The Saxon settlement with its tiny church was finally abandoned after the Exeter turnpike was re-routed through Morcombelake. Carved corbels, said to depict the unlucky couple, are now in the Dorchester museum.

Overlooking the 18 mile-long Chesil Beach from the Isle of Portland

Chesil Beach & Abbotsbury

Britain's longest barrier beach, a pilgrim's chapel, swannery and attractive village all combined in a single walk

What to expect:
Generally good paths after short stretch of shingle, grass descent from Chapel Hill

Distance/time: 8 kilometres/ 5 miles (including Swannery). Allow 2 to 3 hours

Start: Beach car park, Buller's Lane (charge)

Grid ref: SY 560 846

Map: Ordnance Survey Explorer OL15: Purbeck & South Dorset

After the walk: Pubs and cafés in Abbotsbury as well as cafés at the Swannery and the start

Walk outline

The walk begins behind the high shingle bank of Chesil Beach, shortly turning inland and skirting Chapel Hill towards Abbotsbury. There is then a climb to the ancient hilltop chapel before descending beyond to the Swannery, which overlooks the head of The Fleet. Heading to the village the route passes a thatched tithe barn, the remains of St Peter's Abbey and St Nicholas' Church. The way back rises around the southern flank of Chapel Hill, giving the opportunity for another look at Chesil Beach before returning to the car park.

Launching from the shingle

Chesil Beach

Running for almost 18 miles between West Bay and Portland, Chesil Beach is the longest shingle bank in the country. It is thought to be debris washed in by rising sea levels and augmented by subsequent cliff erosion. Ground by the waves, longshore drift pushes the stones eastwards, sorting the pebbles and moving the larger ones towards Portland. At its eastern end the bank has trapped a brackish pool that attracts many birds, including the Abbotsbury swans.

Abbotsbury swannery

The Walk

1. Leave the far end of the **car park** and turn left behind the high **shingle bank**. The going soon improves as a path develops, shortly turning inland as a track. After 1 kilometre, at a fork, bear right through a gate and keep going, passing another junction before reaching a final junction behind a **stone barn**.

2. Go right through a kissing gate and bear right with the broader path that climbs the hill to **St Catherine's Chapel**, protected from the grazing sheep by gated railings.

3. Leaving the enclosure, turn right and walk down hill towards the distant Isle of Portland. Lower down, **Chapel Coppice** appears. Bear left to skirt the trees, picking up a clearer path that drops to a **stone marker**.

4. Take the path ahead, going over a stile to cross a narrow field. Continue over a second stile to emerge through trees onto a drive. The entrance to the **Swannery** lies just to the right.

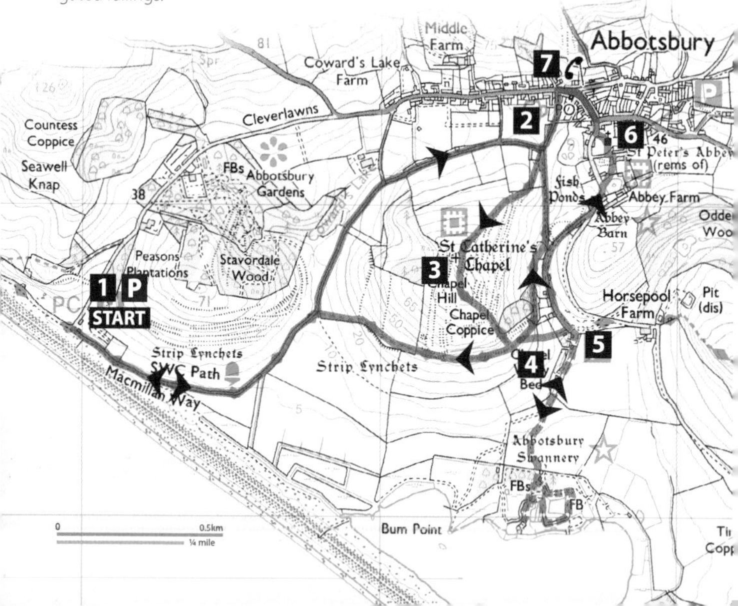

Storm surge: *Surf crashes onto the steeply banked pebbles along Chesil Beach*

Abbotsbury's nesting colony of mute swans is unique and was established by the Benedictine monks of St Peter's shortly after the abbey was founded. The birds, which today can number in excess of 600 with around 150 breeding pairs, provided a ready source of meat for the abbot's table. After the abbey's dissolution in 1539, it was bought by Sir Guy Strangeways, whose descendants still hold the Ilchester Estate and continue to manage the swannery.

As you will hear, particularly at feeding time, mute swans are not silent. However, they do not make as much noise as other species. Native to Europe, they are Britain's only resident swan, with whooper and the smaller Bewick's swans arriving only to overwinter from Iceland and Siberia respectively. One of the largest flying birds, those here are free to fly away, but The Fleet offers an ideal habitat in the generally calm water with plenty of aquatic weed on which they naturally feed. Their diet here is supplement by the daily distribution of grain, the feeding session being a popular attraction for visitors.

Shipwreck shore: *Chesil Beach is a stunning 18-mile long shingle bank or 'barrier beach'*

5. The onward route, however is left. After 500 metres, join with another lane and continue a little further to a bend in front of the **Tithe Barn**.

The huge, thatched barn was built around 1390 and stood at the centre of the monastery farm. It is one of the largest surviving tithe barns in the country and reflects the abbey's medieval prosperity.

Immediately round the bend, leave along a track on the right. Passing the old **millpond**, bear left up to the **church** past the ruin of **St Peter's Abbey**. Wind round beneath the church's tower to find the entrance porch on the north side.

6. Exit the **churchyard** through a gate at the north west corner and turn right into the **village**. Keep ahead along **Market Street**, curving left past the **Ilchester Arms** for another 100 metres to find a track signed off on the left beside **Chapel Lane Stores**.

7. Follow the track to a junction below **Chapel Hill** (Point 2) and, as before go through the kissing gate in front. However, this time, as the way splits, keep with the lower branch beside a wall. Shortly approaching a **bridge**,

bear off right to continue briefly above a **stream** to a fork. Keep with the higher path above a belt of trees to a gate and stile. Pass through **Chapel Coppice**, emerging at the far side to reach the **stone marker** passed earlier (Point 4).

Now, keep ahead with the **coast path**, rising around the flank of Chapel Hill. Through a later gate, carry on beside a fence to a stile. Cross out onto a track and go left, retracing your steps back to the car park, to complete the walk. ♦

An ancient abbey

Founded under the Benedictine order during the 11th century, the abbey of St Peter's former prosperity is reflected in the great thatched tithe barn still standing by the abbey ruins. After the Dissolution, the monastery was plundered for its stone, but St Catherine's Chapel, built on the hill as a retreat for the monk's has survived. Dedicated to the patron saint of virgins, it became a place of pilgrimage, with local girls coming to pray for a husband

Portland Bill's red-and-white striped working lighthouse is 135 feet high

Portland Bill

Dorset's southern-most point, two lighthouses, abandoned coastal quarries and an intriguing coastline

What to expect:
Easy paths and tracks throughout, little climbing

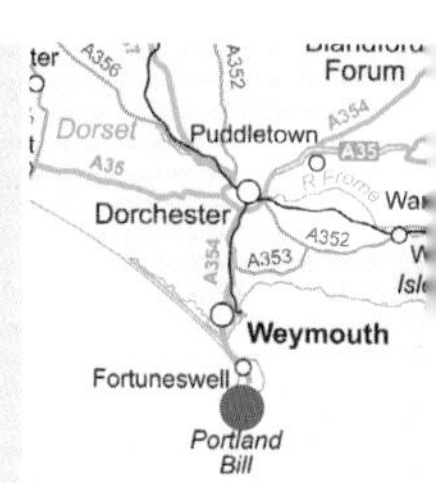

Distance/time: 6.5 kilometres/ 4 miles. Allow 2 to 2½ hours

Start: Portland Bill car park (pay and display)

Grid ref: SY 677 685

Map: Ordnance Survey Explorer OL15: Purbeck & South Dorset

After the walk: The Lobster Pot Restaurant, Portland Bill DT5 2JT
01305 820242 | www.lobsterpotrestaurantportland.co.uk

Walk outline

Beginning by Portland Bill lighthouse, the walk skirts an MOD facility before crossing open grassland above the western cliffs. Beyond a former lighthouse, the route cuts inland around field enclosures to emerge onto the road at the edge of Southwell. Another track drops past old quarries to the eastern coast, where the way swings south through abandoned quarry floors. The last leg winds past the Bill's beach huts back to the point.

Pulpit Rock

Isle of Portland

Tied to mainland Dorset by the tenuous ribbon of Chesil Beach, the Isle of Portland is famous for its fine, white limestone, which has been used for some of Britain's greatest buildings such as St Paul's Cathedral, the Cenotaph and Liverpool's Cunard Building. The stone was of such exceptional architectural quality that it was exported abroad, and can be found as far away as New Zealand's Auckland War Memorial Museum. Ships have taken refuge in the island's shelter since Roman times and the harbour was a Royal Navy base until 1995. One of the largest in the world, it was begun in the mid-19th century using convict labour housed in what was initially a temporary prison at Grove above Portland's East Cliff.

Early gentian

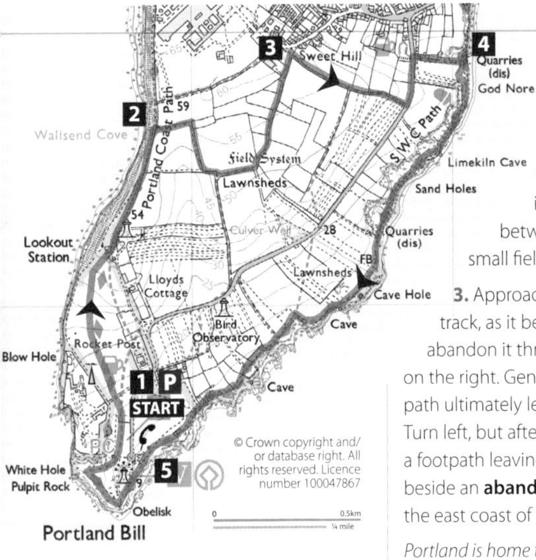

Portland Bill

The Walk

1. From the top of the **car park**, head out on a grassy swathe across the open down, crossing a track and continuing past the **MOD facility** to join the coast. The way continues above unseen cliffs towards the **National Coastwatch lookout station**. Carry on along the coast path, passing the old **high lighthouse** where the view opens north to the impressive sheer cliffs of Blacknor.

2. After some 400 metres, watch for a **stone marker** indicating a path off to the right. Head inland beside a paddock, swinging first right and later left. As the track then bends right again, keep ahead on a lesser track to meet an old, **walled lane**. Follow it left, meandering between a patchwork of small fields and paddocks.

3. Approaching the end of the track, as it becomes concrete, abandon it through a kissing gate on the right. Gently losing height, the path ultimately leads through to a road. Turn left, but after 200 metres cross to a footpath leaving on the right. It runs beside an **abandoned quarry** to meet the east coast of the island.

Portland is home to some of England's rarest flowers and is internationally important for the mosses, lichens and liverworts that grow here. Amongst the flowers to look out for are autumn lady's tresses and Portland spurge. The profusion of flowers growing on the island attracts numerous insects including the adonis and chalk hill blue butterflies.

4. After wandering a little way to the left for the **view**, turn around and follow the **coast path** south through a succession of **old quarry workings**. Further along, standing on the edge of the cliff is a **wooden derrick**, once used

Rock bands: *The lighthouse and Trinity House obelisk on Portland Bill*

for lowering stone to waiting ships. After a while, another derrick is seen, this one perched above a sea cave. Continuing along the coast, the way winds past some of the **wooden chalets** that have sprung up on this side of the Bill. Towards the far end is a third derrick, which is now used by local fishermen.

5. Carry on past the **Lobster Pot Restaurant** and the **lighthouse** to a three-sided tapering **obelisk**, a navigation marker erected in 1844. The path continues around the rugged point to a flat apron of cliff overlooking **Pulpit Rock**. Forced inland by the MOD perimeter fence, the path returns you to the car park to complete the walk. ♦

Lighthouses on Portland Bill

Treacherous currents and unseen shoals have long wrought havoc to shipping along this coast, but despite the protestations of the Wareham townsfolk, it was 1716 before two coal-fired lights were privately built on the Bill. Replaced in 1869, they were eventually superseded by the present single tower in 1906, which stands 41 metres high and is visible for 25 nautical miles. The old low light now serves as a bird observatory.

The pebble and shingle beach at Ringstead Bay

Ringstead Bay

Undulating coastal downs and slumping cliffs lead past an unusual church back to a popular beach

What to expect: *Undulating field and coastal paths, with a sustained but not overly steep climb*

Distance/time: 7.25 kilometres/ 4½ miles. Allow 2½ to 3 hours

Start: Ringstead Bay car park (charge)

Grid ref: SY 751 815

Map: Ordnance Survey Explorer OL15: Purbeck & South Dorset

After the walk: The Kiosk (beach cafe), Ringstead DT2 8NG

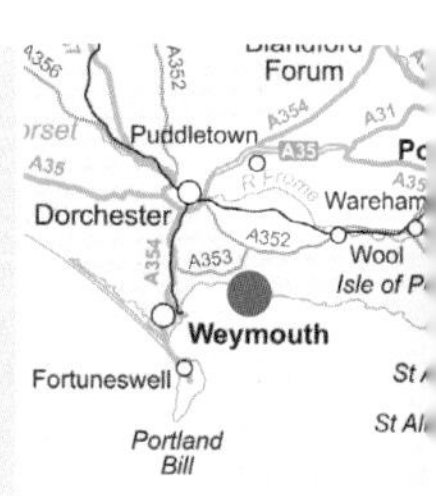

Walk outline

Beginning along the coast past the site of an abandoned medieval village, the route soon turns inland through woods. After climbing onto the downs, the way continues beside open fields to a small group of ancient tumuli. Turning out to the cliffs, a short walk east reveals views past Bat's Head and Durdle Door, before heading back past White Nothe and above a long run of slumping undercliff. The gradual descent to the beach at Ringstead gives views over Weymouth Bay.

Ringstead

Ringstead's medieval village, which clustered around a small church, was abandoned during the 14th century after the Black Death swept through the area, its surviving population dispersing to find a better living. The house platforms and foundations have disappeared beneath coastal fields and today's settlement comprises a handful of modern houses and a small holiday site. The beach remains a local beauty spot, with fine sand revealed beyond the shingle at low tide and safe bathing in the lee of an offshore reef. The area is known for its butterflies, birds and wildflowers, with plenty to see at most times of the year.

Ringstead Bay

Bee orchid

The Walk

1. Leaving the **car park**, turn left towards the beach, swinging right at the bottom past a **small parking area** and some houses scattered along the coast. Reaching the end of the track, branch left to continue with the **coast path** over a **bridge** into trees. *The open fields then to your right are the site of the abandoned medieval village.*

Dropping to a junction within more trees, go right, shortly reaching a small **bridge**. Cross and follow the path through woodland before emerging onto a broad track. Walk right, keeping right further on and eventually meeting a lane. Go right again for 400 metres to find a path leaving over a stile on the left.

2. Walk away at the field edge, crossing a **stiled bridge** into a larger field. Head away, gently gaining height along a vague trod, passing an occasional waypost to reach a gate and stile at the far end. Cross a track and continue in the same direction. At the far end of the field, go over a stile (not the nearby gate) and climb, now more steeply, onto **South Down**.

3. Joining a track by a **National Trust information panel**, walk right through a gate. After some 600 metres, as the track bends right, leave through the gate ahead, not over the stile beside it.

4. Still rising, the old track climbs on past a **large, thatched barn** eventually passing a couple of distinctive **tumuli** over to the right.

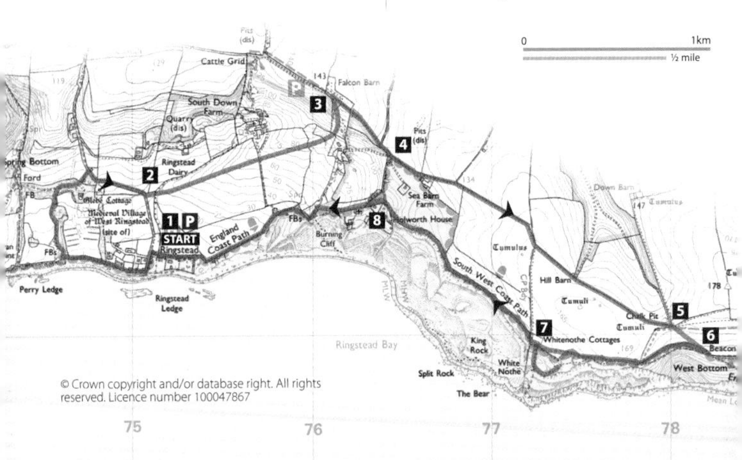

Up on the downs: *Overlooking Ringstead Bay from high on the coast path*

Chaldon Down has seen settlement since the Bronze Age, with several burial barrows and tumuli scattered around the highpoints. Less visible are the vague outlines of ancient field systems and it is believed that a Roman vineyard occupied one of the deep valleys running to the north.

5. Walk forward to a gate and bear away half-right, dropping across the down to a gate in the bottom fence. A short distance to the left is a prominent **navigation beacon**, paired with another some 600 metres inland on top of the hill.

They were erected during the 19th century as transit markers to aid the navigation of shipping on the roads around Portland's massive harbour.

6. Having enjoyed the view to the east past **Bat's Head**, turn around and head back towards **Ringstead**, in time reaching a terrace of former **coastguard cottages** at **White Nothe**.

Swimmers' delight: *An offshore reef protects the pebble beach at Ringstead Bay*

7. A path off to the left past a **wartime lookout** doubles back above the cliffs to a viewpoint by the **'White Nose'**, but the 'Smugglers' path down the cliffs is not recommended. Return to the coast path and continue west above the **undercliff** — a vast confused area of ongoing landslip. Towards the far end, the path descends past **Burning Cliff**, so called because of its bituminous shales, which spontaneously ignited and smouldered underground for many years during the 19th century.

8. The way drops to a track. Cross to the path opposite, which soon rejoins the track beside the tiny wooden church of **St Catherine's by the Sea**. *Built in 1926 to serve this isolated community, its treasure is an engraved window by Simon Whistler to commemorate a local farmer, Donald Wilkinson, and Rachel Nickell, brutally murdered on Wimbledon Common.* Continue with the track for a further 1.2 kilometres, passing occasional **cottages** and a **small holiday site** before meeting a lane. The car park is then a short distance to the right and so completes the walk.

Then still in its infancy, radar was vital

to the defence of Britain during the early months of the Second World War. A chain of stations was established along the country's south and east coasts to give early warning of the approach of Nazi aircraft. The 15th September 1940 was a turning point, when 185 enemy planes were shot down, and the threat of imminent invasion began to recede. One such station was at Ringstead, the remains of its bunker still standing beside the Coast Path near the end of the walk. ♦

Moonfleet

The treacherous path zigzagging down the cliffs at White Nothe is said to be the smuggler's escape route described in the gripping, late 19th-century children's novel Moonfleet. *Illicit cargoes carried over from France and beyond were landed on lonely beaches to be spirited away before the Revenue Officers arrived. White Nothe's clifftop coastguard cottages were built only in the early 1900s, but the service was originally set up in 1822 to prevent smuggling.*

Durdle Door is one of the most famous features on Dorset's Jurassic Coast

Lulworth Cove

A stunning walk exploring two of Dorset's best-known and impressive geological wonders

What to expect:
Some steep climbs and generally good underfoot, although the section around Dungy Head can be slippery after rain

Distance/time: 7.25 kilometres/ 4½ miles. Allow 3 to 3½ hours

Start: Lulworth Cove car park (pay and display)

Grid ref: SY 821 801

Map: Ordnance Survey Explorer OL15: Purbeck & South Dorset

After the walk: Pubs and cafés at Heritage Centre and Lulworth Cove

Walk outline

From the car park, the walk's outward leg skirts behind Hambury Tout to Durdle Door car park. Staying high, it winds across Newlands Warren before dropping along the deep valley of Scratchy Bottom to the coast. There is then an optional climb onto Swyre Head for the view to Bat's Head before heading back along the coast to Durdle Door. The way then climbs over the seaward shoulder of Hambury Tout but, rather than return directly to the car park, it detours over Dungy Head to Stair Hole and the western horn of Lulworth Cove.

Above Durdle Door

Lulworth Cove

The bay at Lulworth is a textbook example of cove formation. A powerful river, created by melting glaciers some 12,000 years ago, forced a narrow gap through the coastal hard Purbeck and Portland limestone strata, which had been tipped upright by ancient continental collision. The sea flooded in to erode the softer clays and sandstones behind, wave refraction creating the perfect cove shape we see today. Although the high chalk cliffs backing the bay are also relatively hard, waves undercut the base causing periodic collapse, and are the reason why the coast path to the east has been diverted inland.

Fossil forest, Lulworth

Iconic shore: *The shelving shingle beach and natural limestone arch at Durdle Door*

The Walk

1. Guided by a sign to 'Durdle Door and Ringstead', walk up to the top of the **overflow car park**. Through the gate, immediately turn off right to follow a grass path over the shoulder of **Hambury Tout**. Reaching a junction by a gate, keep ahead above a fence around the flank of the hill, heading towards the **Durdle Door Holiday Park**. Continue through gates, eventually emerging at the entrance to a **car park**.

2. Go left towards a gate at the bottom of the parking. Swing right before and follow a grass swathe beside the car park to a gate at the top. Keep going towards another gate at the crest of the hill.

3. Instead of going through, turn right, initially beside the fence, but then shortly curving away to pass through another gate onto a track. Go right for some 20 metres before turning off sharp left on a path that falls through gorse and bracken undergrowth beside the holiday park. Continue through a

stand of pine, swinging right and left at the bottom to emerge onto another track. Follow it left gently down through **Scratchy Bottom** out to the coast.

4. To the right, the **coast path** climbs steeply to the top of **Swyre Head**, the effort compensated by a fine view of Bat's Head and on along the coast to the west. Having admired the view retrace your steps to (**Point 4**) and climb the less steep path over the headland to **Durdle Door**, where there is a viewing area and paths to the shore in each of the adjacent bays.

5. Rejoin the coast path to climb away from Durdle Door. Towards the top, turn through a gate on the right, the way signed to 'Lulworth Cove'. The path runs high across grassy slopes above the cliffs, eventually becoming paved and descending towards the car park.

6. However, part-way down, watch for a lesser path leaving sharp right, which slants back across the steep slope to a gate near the head of the valley. Briefly follow the narrow ridge left but then drop right to a path climbing from St Oswald's Bay. Cross to the path opposite, keeping right and left at successive forks to climb onto **Dungy Head**.

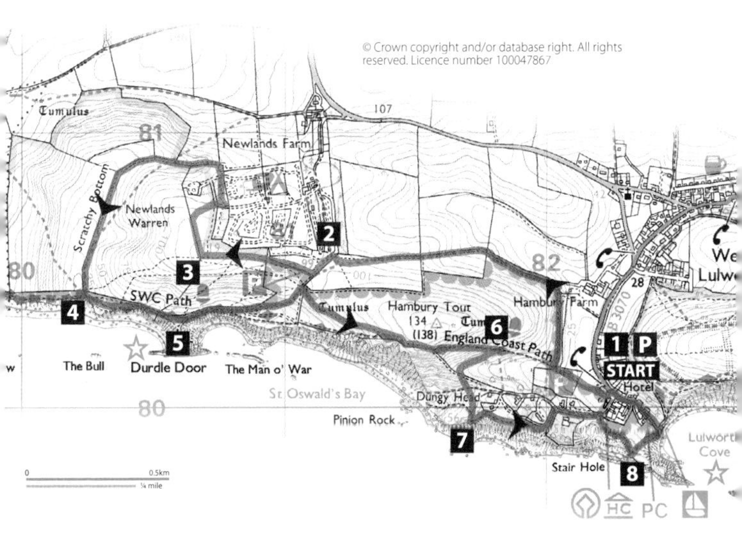

Perfect circle?: *Lulworth Cove is protected by a band of resistant coastal limestone*

7. A narrow path leads away to the left above a line of rugged cliffs, eventually turned inland in front of a small **wildlife reserve**. The path falls between trees and a couple of gardens to emerge onto a drive. Follow it down right, passing through a gate. Just beyond, take a path off on the right, which leads to a viewpoint above **Stair Hole**.

Next door to Lulworth, Stair Hole is a younger version of Lulworth Cove, where the sea has only relatively recently broken through the outer bands of limestone and is just starting to erode the softer clays behind. Impressive are the natural rock arches through which the sea floods and the intricate folding of the rock strata, known as the 'Lulworth Crumple'.

The way continues to a second lookout over **Lulworth Cove**.

8. From there, the path drops to the head of the cove and beach. Walk up the lane back to the **car park** to complete the walk.

Dubbed Lulwind in Thomas Hardy's novel, Far From the Madding Crowd, *Lulworth was the scene of Sergeant Troy's supposed drowning after he swam out between its*

enclosing pillars to the open sea. But like a bad penny, he turns up again to wreak havoc upon the tragic tale.

The secluded cove was ideal for smugglers, who regularly landed cargoes of spirits, wine and other goods from France, but the Revenue Men were never far behind and in the early 18th century, Lulworth was the scene of a long and frantic battle as the King's men tried to seize the barrels being brought ashore. ♦

Lulworth Ranges

The coast and downs east of Lulworth are part of the Armoured Fighting Vehicles Gunnery School. Requisitioned in 1943 when its inhabitants were evacuated. Yet, despite operational use, the surrounding countryside has become a haven for wildlife. Tyneham's church and school, now a museum, survive and, although off limits during training, there is generally weekend and school holiday access along designated paths and to the abandoned village of Tyneham.

Wave-cut platforms of shale shimmer under a dawn sea

Kimmeridge Ledges

A fine walk to an impressive tumulus, returning above extensive wave-cut platforms and a curious tower

What to expect:
Generally good paths, but with a steep, grass descent from Swyre Hill which can be slippery

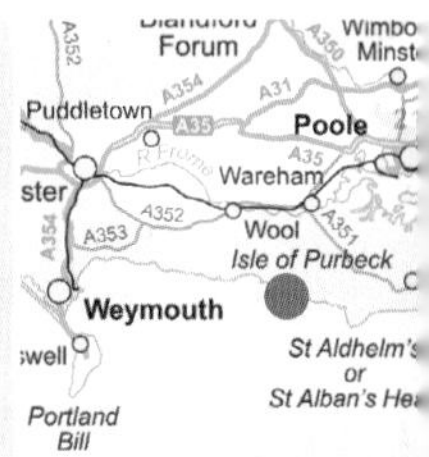

Distance/time: 9 kilometres/ 5½ miles. Allow 3 to 3½ hours

Start: Kimmeridge Bay car park (charge)

Grid ref: SY 910 788

Map: Ordnance Survey Explorer OL15: Purbeck & South

After the walk: Clavell's Café & Restaurant, Kimmeridge BH20 5PE 01929 480701 | www.clavell'scafe.co.uk

Walk outline

Leaving the coastal car park by Gaulter Gap, the way rises through fields to the village where there's refreshment and a fossil museum. Climbing beyond onto the downs, the route continues to Swyre Head, where an impressive tumulus provides a grandstand lookout along the coast. After dropping steeply off the hill to the coast at Rope Lake Head, the walk returns above Kimmeridge Ledges to the restored Clavell Tower before dropping to the head of the bay where there is access to the beach.

Kimmeridge waterfall

Kimmeridge

Kimmeridge has given its name to the underlying clays that form its cliffs, which contain bands of bituminous shale. The rock was worked by Iron Age settlers to produce decorative amulets, but the Romans realised a more practical use as fuel. Industrial exploitation began in the 16th century with attempts to produce alum and glass, and Clavell, who owned the Smedmore estate, tried to establish a port, but all came to nought. By the 19th century, the shale was being used to produce oil-based products such as dye, naphtha and even gas. The oil well, overlooking the bay, was sunk in 1959 and has been producing ever since.

Ammonite in shale

The Walk

1. Begin beside the **toilets** in the lower parking area and head west towards Lulworth. As the track swings right, keep ahead on grass, sticking with the **coast path** as it delves through vegetation and below a **second parking area**. At the far end, leave the coast path and swing right to a tarmac drive. Go left past the **small settlement**, ignoring a stile on the right, but as the track then swings left, take a short field track off right, signed to 'Kimmeridge'.

2. Entering a field, go right and left with the perimeter. Continue in successive fields, remaining by the right boundary until you eventually reach a couple of gates on the right. Take the first, crossing a **footbridge** into another field. Head away at the left edge, crossing out over a stile to meet a lane.

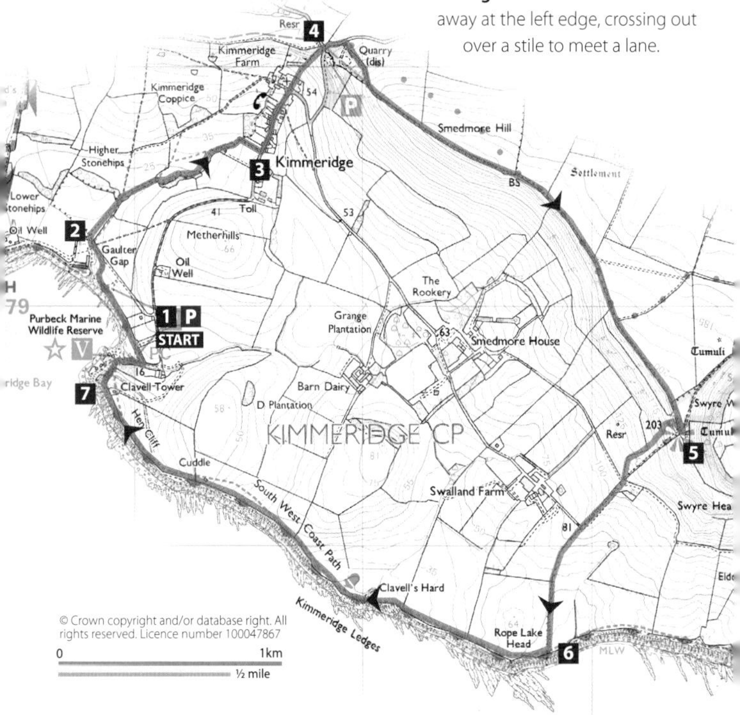

Slow tide: *Long-exposure creates a misty sheen on the rocks at Kimmeridge Bay*

3. Turn left through the **village**, passing **Clavell's Café** and **The Etches Collection fossil museum**. As the lane then sharply bends, climb ahead into the **churchyard**. Walk through and continue straight uphill in the field beyond to a stile at the top, emerging onto a junction of lanes.

4. Follow the lane opposite for 100 metres to find a **stony track** leaving on the right. Climbing steadily away, it opens an expanding view along the coast. Carry on through a succession of gates, the way eventually levelling to reveal the sweep of Swyre Head in front. Stride on to the **end of the ridge**, passing a **trig column** to an **impressive tumulus** just beyond, from which a panorama stretches all the way from the Isle of Portland to the Needles on the Isle of Wight.

There are actually two Swyre Heads in Dorset, the other on the coast just west of Durdle Door and attained on Walk 5.

The one here set back from the cliffs, however, has the distinction of being

Heavenly path: *Low light illuminates Clavell Tower above Kimmeridge Bay*

the highest point of the Purbeck Hills. It is topped by a Bronze Age bowl barrow, which sufficiently elevates its relative height for it to be included in the list of 'Marilyn' hills, that is, 150 metres above its surroundings. The top of the barrow is capped by a stone slab, which is thought to have been the base of a 19th-century windmill.

5. Head back towards the trig column, watching for a stile on the left from which a permissive footpath is signed to 'Rope Lake Head'. A steep, and occasionally stepped path picks its way down the flank of the hill, in time leading to a gate. Now in a field, continue beside the left boundary, following it around to a stile in the corner. Go briefly left and then through a gate on the right. A **farm track** leads on down the hill, but where it later bends right, leave through a gate on the left. Walk on beside the right-hand field edge, emerging over a stile at the bottom onto the coast path.

6. The return route is to the right. At first, all the views are behind you, but later, cresting a rise, the run of cliffs to Lulworth Cove and beyond appear

ahead. The way undulates on to **Clavell Tower,** which stands some 25 metres inland from its original site, the foundation of which is still visible.

7. Beyond the tower, the path drops steeply down a long **flight of steps** that leads to the end of the lane above the bay. The car park is then a short distance up to the right, to complete the walk. ♦

Clavell Tower

Commissioned in 1830 by Rev. Clavell of Smedmore, the four-storey tower affords a spectacular panorama of the coast. Thomas Hardy was a regular visitor when courting his sweetheart Eliza Nicholl, and it featured in PD James' novel The Black Tower. *But as the 21st century dawned, the building was in danger of toppling as the cliffs were eroded. A public appeal and Lottery Grant secured the tower's future and it was dismantled and rebuilt 25 metres further back.*

Chapman's Pool is rich in fossil ammonites and bivalves

St Aldhelm's Head

Fine views from the southernmost point of this corner of Dorset, where a tiny chapel stands on the remote clifftop

What to expect:
Lane, field and coastal paths; a sustained, steep climb

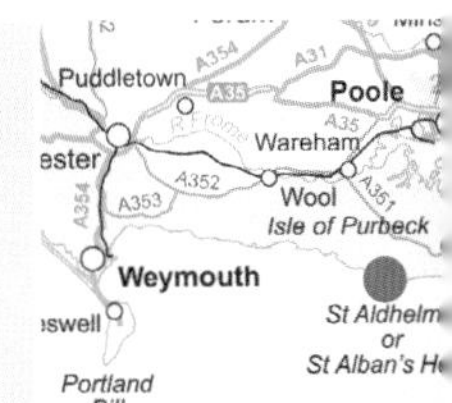

Distance/time: : 9 kilometres/ 5½ miles. Allow 2½ to 3 hours

Start: Village car park, Worth Matravers (charge)

Grid ref: SY 973 776

Map: Ordnance Survey Explorer OL15: Purbeck & South Dorset

Refreshment: Square and Compass, Worth Matravers BH19 3LF| 01929 439229; Worth Matravers Tea & Supper Room, Worth Matravers BH19 3LQ | 01929 439 368

Walk outline

After following the lane west through the village to Renscombe, the way crosses fields to gain the high cliffs above the inlet of Chapman's Pool. Turning south, an easy trek over Emmetts Hill precedes an abrupt descent and climb through the foot of a deep valley broaching the cliff. Back on the cliff top, the path rounds the headland past St Aldhelm's Chapel and a National Coastwatch lookout station to continue to Winspit. The route progresses over East Man to Seacombe before rising inland up a valley back to Worth Matravers.

Radar memorial sculpture

St Aldhelm's Chapel

The tiny chapel on the coast dedicated to St Aldhelm dates from the 12th century, but was rebuilt around 1870 having become derelict. It stands within a low earthwork enclosure, possibly the site of an early hermitage, but the building may originally have been used as a watchtower for Corfe Castle, and evidence suggests it was once topped with a beacon and used as a navigation aid for mariners. The medieval grave of a woman was found nearby and the carved slab that covered it can be seen in the porch of St Nicholas' Church in the village.

Lulworth skipper butterfly

The Walk

1. Leaving the **car park**, turn right to the **Square and Compass** and go right again, keeping with the main lane as it winds past the **duck pond**, **tea room** and **church** through the **village**. Continue beyond for a further kilometre, before swinging left in front of **Renscombe Farm** to a **car park**.

2. Turn into the car park to leave through a gate on the left, and strike half-right across a crop field. Continue between more fields beyond to emerge over a stile onto the coast path above **Chapman's Pool**.

3. The way lies to the left, shortly passing a small **memorial garden** dedicated to the Royal Marines.

During the late 19th century, a lifeboat was briefly stationed at Chapman's Pool, but its remoteness and continual landslides led to it being abandoned after only 13 years. On the cliffs above is a small memorial to the Royal Marines, established after the IRA bombing of the RM Barracks at Deal in which 11 marines were killed and 21 others

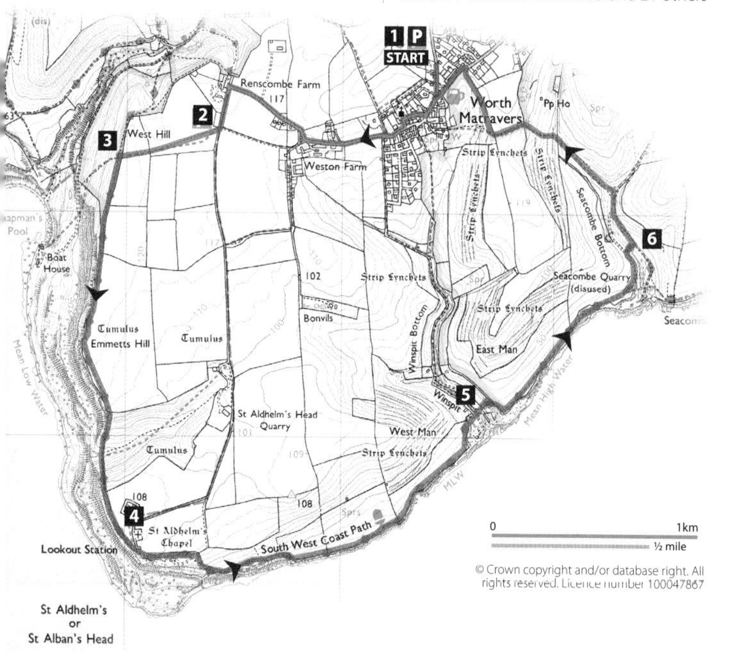

Remote church: *St Aldhelm's Norman chapel sits within a circular earthen enclosure*

injured. It now remembers all Marines who have been lost in conflicts since 1945 and overlooks a training area used by the Marines during the Second World War.

Carry on over a stile, the chapel on **St Aldhelm's Head** now appearing in front. However, the intervening path drops steeply down a **long flight of steps** to cross the foot of a valley, climbing equally steeply beyond to regain the cliff top.

4. After exploring **St Aldhelm's Chapel** and perhaps visiting the **Coastwatch station**, continue around the point past a dish-shaped **sculpture** remembering the pioneering radar work undertaken here during World War Two. Forking right, the path falls to run at a lower level to **Winspit**. Passing above **Winspit quarries**, the path turns inland and drops down steps to a track along the valley.

5. At the bottom, go right towards the **quarry floor** and then almost immediately left to climb back onto

Bat cave: *Massive limestone columns support the roof at Winspit quarry*

the cliffs. Eventually, approaching **Seacombe**, there is a **quarry pit** on the left, the way then soon turning above the **main quarry** and descending **steps** through a thicket once again into a valley.

Stone was first quarried here by the Romans, who exploited the many outcrops of Purbeck limestone. Although less suited for outdoor work, as weathering causes flaking, it can be highly polished to resemble marble and was prized for decorative work. Although lapsing during the Dark Ages, the industry revived with the great age of medieval cathedral and church building, as did the quarrying and mining of Portland limestone, which was used for both construction and fine paving flags.

Many of the quarries were abandoned during the 1930s, but that at Winspit was subsequently used to house air and naval defences, while the rubble was removed to build wartime airfields. It has been since served as a film location for Blake's 7 *and* Doctor Who, *amongst others.*

6. To explore the quarry go right, but otherwise turn left on a broad grass track. At a fork, take the left branch

waymarked to 'Worth'. Through a gate at the top, carry on past old **strip lynchets** off to the left and then up steps to a gate. Keep going across pasture to another gate, through which turn right. Keep your height above a grassy fold, eventually turning into the field corner where a gate leads out onto a lane. Turn left into **Worth Matravers**, finally going right at the **Square and Compass** back to the car park to complete the walk. ♦

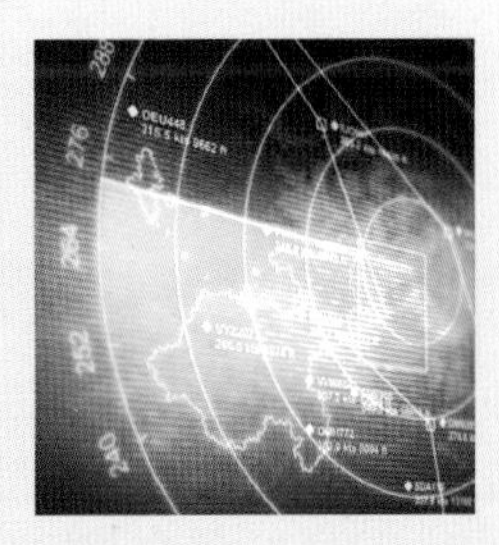

Wartime Radar

Rudimentary radar existed before the war, but the race was on to improve accuracy and portability. The development team was stationed at Worth from 1940 to 1942, taking advantage of the flat clifftop headland and being less vulnerable to enemy attack than the original Suffolk base. By 1942, some 2,000 personnel were engaged in the top secret work. An RAF radar station remained operational here until 1976.

Waves wash over the rock platform at Dancing Ledge

Dancing Ledge

A stunning stretch of coast, abandoned quarries and mines and views to Portland Bill and the Isle of Wight

What to expect:
Tracks, field and coastal paths

Distance/time: 9.25 kilometres/ 5¾ miles. Allow 2½ to 3 hours

Start: Village car park, Worth Matravers (charge)

Grid ref: SY 973 776

Map: Ordnance Survey Explorer OL15: Purbeck & South Dorset

Refreshment: Square and Compass, Worth Matravers BH193LF 01929 439229 OR Worth Matravers Tea & Supper Room, Worth Matravers BH19 3LQ | 01929 439 368

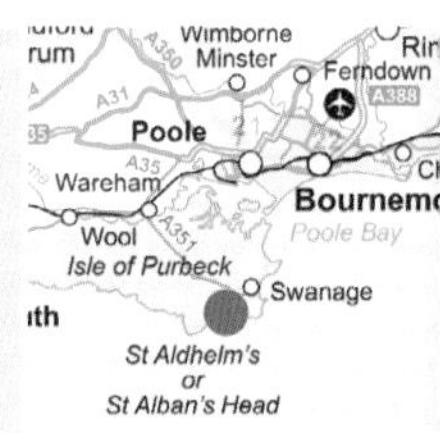

Walk outline

The outward leg follows old paths and lanes between the inland fields past Keates Quarry before turning past the evocatively named Spyway Barn down to the coast. From Dancing Ledge, another former quarry, the route follows the clifftops, passing more old quarries at Hedbury and Seacombe. At Winspit Quarry, the way turns inland, climbing along a deep valley back to the village.

Dancing Ledge

Like that at Durlston, this section of coast has been heavily worked for its fine limestone. Stone was quarried either directly from the cliffs or dug from huge tunnels following the seams of the best stone below ground. The stone was loaded directly onto ships, which could moor beside the quarry floor when the tide was right and, at Dancing Ledge, the wheel tracks to guide the loaded tubs can still be seen.

Intriguing too, seen towards the end of the walk, are long terraces contouring the hillside. Known as strip lynchets, they are the remains of medieval strip fields that were farmed by the villagers.

Dinosaur footprint

Carline thistle and moth

The Walk

1. Head down from the **car park** to the **Square and Compass**, there going left. After 400 metres, at the edge of the village, leave through a gate on the right.

2. A path strikes a diagonal course across the field, continuing through gates over a track on the same line beyond. Joining a field track at the far side, follow it right through another gate and walk on along the **Priest's Way** for 500 metres to find a small gate on the left. A path leads across the field to an enclosure, where **dinosaur tracks** have been uncovered on an old quarry floor.

Dinosaur tracks have been discovered here and at another quarry, a little farther north. They are thought to have been left 140 million years ago by a group of brachiosaurs converging around a waterhole. Massive, long-necked, quadrupeds, they were one of the largest dinosaurs to have lived, growing to around

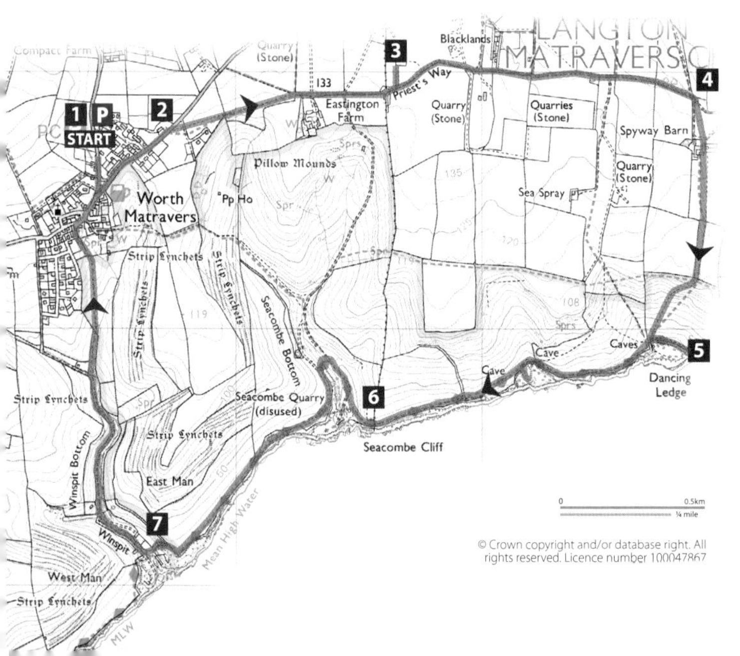

Sea ballet?: *Watching a rising tide 'dance' over the rocks at Dancing Ledge*

25 metres long and weighing up to 50 tonnes. Vegetarians, they browsed the high foliage of trees, consuming over 100 kilograms of fodder each day, but the idea of them wading in lakes to support their weight is no longer considered true; the water pressure on their bodies would have prevented them breathing.

3. Return to the walled track and continue between fields toward Langton Matravers. Over a crossing track, further on by a **working quarry**, the ground begins to fall and a view opens ahead to Swanage and the distant cliffs of the Isle of Wight. Ignore a path then marked off to 'Dancing Ledge', continuing a little further to a crossing path from Langton Matravers.

4. Now, turn right, the way signed to 'Dancing Ledge', following a cut swathe across the meadow. Keep ahead between the buildings at **Spyway Barn** and cross two more meadows before passing through a gate by a **carved cow's head** onto the Open Access land above the coast. Walk briefly right and then bear left

Secret shore: *Steps curve down to Dancing Ledge from the coast path*

on a path that winds to the cliffs below. Over a stile, a stepped path drops to **Dancing Ledge**.

5. Climb back to the stile and go left with the **coast path**, shortly passing behind the **Hedbury quarry**. A path leads down to this one too, where an **old cannon** is mounted on a block of stone. Further west along the coast path, the path winds in above **Seacombe**, dropping to the bottom of the valley. Access to the quarries here is over a stile beside a gate to the left.

6. The onward route, however, follows the track inland, but watch for a path signed to 'Winspit' soon leaving through a gate on the left. Climb steps and skirt behind the quarry to rejoin the coast. Further on, on the right, is a **deep pit** from which stone was removed through a tunnel beneath your feet. Approaching **Winspit**, curve in towards a gate and drop steeply into the valley.

7. Again the quarry is to the left, but the way back follows the track right. After some 800 metres, branch right onto a narrower path and continue beyond its end across a field.

Clearly visible on the hillside above the

path back from Winspit are lynchets, long narrow fields created by Saxon farmers, whose ploughing along the contours left terraced strips that maximised the land available for cultivation.

Leave through a gate at the top, from which a contained path leads into **Worth Matravers**. Carry on up to the main street beside the **duck pond**, there going right and then left back to the **car park** to complete the walk. ♦

Dancing Ledge

So named because the rippling of the waves at mid-tide appears to make the ledge 'dance', Dancing Ledge segued from industrial site to local beauty spot after coastal quarrying ended. One of the last acts of the quarrymen was to cut a basin in the gently sloping ledge, the water replenished with each tide. The rock-pool served as a swimming pool for local schools and among the famous to have bathed here are David Niven and Ian Fleming.

The coast path at Durlston looks out towards the Isle of Wight

Durlston Head

An undemanding coastal walk taking in flower rich meadows and a Victorian pleasure garden

What to expect:
Easy clifftop and downland paths

Distance/time: 4.5 kilometres/ 2¾ miles. Allow 1½ to 2 hours

Start: Durlston Country Park car park (pay and display)

Grid ref: SZ 033 773

Map: Ordnance Survey Explorer OL15: Purbeck & South Dorset

After the walk: Seventhwave restaurant, Durlston Country Park BH19 2JL | 01929 424443 | www.durlston.co.uk

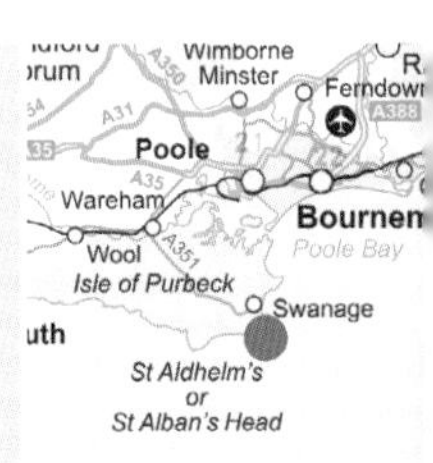

Walk outline

A short walk that begins past the Victorian castle (now a visitor centre and restaurant) and the locally famous Globe. Dropping to the coast, the way continues past Tilly Whim Caves to the lighthouse on Anvil Point. The route carries on with the coast path above a straight run of cliffs before climbing back across rough pasture to return through a series of spectacular wildflower meadows.

Durlston Globe

Durlston Head

From the latter part of the 18th century, Durlston Head was extensively mined for its high quality limestone. However, things changed towards the end of the 19th century, when George Burt developed the headland for living and leisure. He built the Castle as a restaurant, opened the Tilly Whim Caves as an attraction and laid out walks, as well as commissioning the 40-ton limestone Globe and many inscribed plaques, to satisfy the Victorian zeal for education. Opened as a country park in the 1970s, it has become a superb wildlife resource, the clifftop meadows containing almost 600 different species of wildflower which in turn attract countless invertebrates, birds and small mammals.

Field scabious

The Walk

1. From the bottom-left corner of the **car park**, a drive leads down to the **Castle restaurant** and **visitor centre**, paralleling a geological timeline tracing the earth's development over 4.54 billion years. From the **Castle** continue downhill, soon veering right to drop to **the Globe**. A flight of steps beyond leads to the **coast path**. Follow it right above the cliffs to **Tilly Whim Caves**.

The Tilly Whim Caves are not natural, but are the result of mining for Purbeck limestone. The industry finished in 1812 and the caves were subsequently opened as a tourist attraction, but the danger of collapse has made them unsafe and by 1976 they were finally closed. They are now a roost for rare bats such as pipistrelles and noctules.

2. Keep with the coast, passing a pair of **transit towers**, *which, together with another set further along the coast, defined a measured mile used for shipping speed trials.* Climb through a dip to carry on past the **lighthouse** enclosure on **Anvil Point**. Through a gate the path continues onto **National Trust land.** Later, pass a stile in the left fence and walk through a gap in a wall to reach a second stile.

3. Leave the coast path there, bearing right on a trod that slants up the hillside. Higher up, watch for it swinging back for the final pull. Soon merging with a broader trod, carry on to reach the wall you crossed earlier. Through a gap, keep going at the edge of rough grazing, shortly joining another trod to a kissing

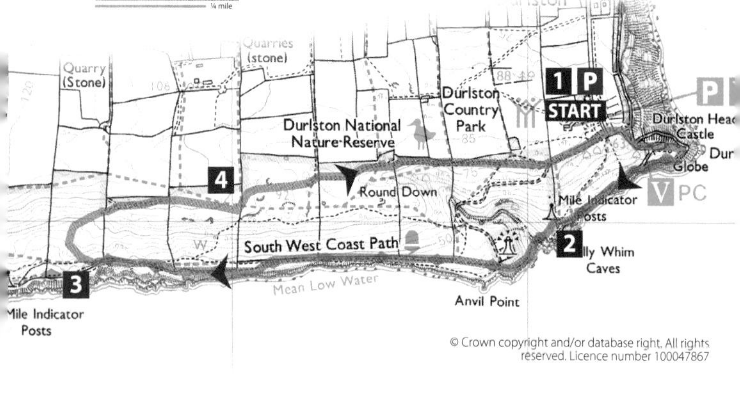

Clifftop sentinel: *The coast path rises steadily past Anvil Point lighthouse*

gate into the **Durlston National Nature Reserve**.

4. Ignoring the path signed off to the left to 'California Farm', go through the gate and bear left (not sharp left). Fork left again where it later splits, shortly winding through a thicket to another gate. Carry on with the main trod, crossing a five-bar gate and stile and rising gently to gain a view to the lighthouse. Beyond another gate, the path then loosely parallels a wall to the left, ultimately joining a drive from the lighthouse. Follow the drive ahead back to the car park to complete the walk. ♦

Durlston's Orchids

Amongst the hundreds of plants flowering on Durlston's chalk grasslands are nine species of orchid. Perhaps the most eye-catching are the early spider and bee orchids. The former (which only resembles, and has nothing to do with spiders) is a nationally scarce species, flowering in April and May. Bee orchids, however, have evolved to mimic their pollinator, the Mediterranean Eucera bee. But this far north, the flowers are self-pollinating.

Lit by a low evening light, Old Harry is reflected in the sea

Old Harry Rocks

A curious boulder isolated on open heath and flower-rich downs lead to Dorset's most spectacular sea stacks

What to expect:
A longer walk on clear paths and tracks, short sections on road and beside unguarded cliffs

Distance/time: 11¼ kilometres/ 7 miles. Allow 3 to 4 hours

Start: Studland village

Grid ref: SZ 037825

Map: Ordnance Survey Explorer OL15: Purbeck & South Dorset

Refreshment: Bankes Arms, Studland BH19 3AU | 01929 450225 | www.bankesarms.com

Walk outline

The walk begins by Studland's ancient church, winding beyond the village onto Godlingston Heath, where it passes the impressive Agglestone boulder. After crossing a golf course and a couple of roads, the way climbs onto Ballard Down, following its long ridge before descending past The Pinnacles to Handfast Point and Old Harry Rocks. The return follows coastal woodland back above Studland Bay to the village, from which there is access to the beach.

Old Harry Rocks

There was a time when the chalk of Purbeck Down formed a continuous ridge all the way out to what is now the Isle of Wight. But rapid melting of vast ice sheets at the end of the last glacial period released unimaginable quantities of water, which swept away the intervening land. The erosion continues with the pounding waves, cutting caves through the cliffs, which eventually collapse to leave dramatic stacks. These in turn are gradually worn away and will also crumble into the sea. In the 18th century, Old Harry was still firmly attached to the land, and in 1896, his first 'Wife' collapsed to leave only a stump. The same process is taking place 15 miles away at the Needles, where one of the needle-shaped stacks named Lot's Wife collapsed during a storm in 1764.

Old Harry's 'Wife'

Male sand lizard

The Walk

1. Leaving the **car park** turn left and immediately left again on a path to **St Nicholas' Church**.

The village church, dedicated to St Nicholas, was founded by the Saxons but destroyed in the 9th century by Viking coastal raiders. It was rebuilt soon after the Norman Conquest, an austere-looking building with a low central tower that was probably intended to have been higher, for it barely clears the nave and its builders settled for a saddleback roof instead. But, the plain exterior is relieved by a succession of animated carvings decorating the corbels, where the stonemasons let rip with imagination and saucy humour. Amongst the animals, birds and other figures there's a sheelagh-na-gig and her male counterpart as well as a couple, unashamedly copulating. Inside is equally interesting, with finely carved capitals and arch mouldings as well as traces of the painted decoration that would once have adorned the walls.

Pass through the **churchyard** and on along another path from its western end out to a lane. Go right to a crossroads and continue along **Heath Green Road** opposite.

2. After 200 metres turn off right along a bridleway marked to 'Godlingston Heath'. Ignoring side paths, keep with the main trail, which eventually narrows to reach a crossing path. Turn right.

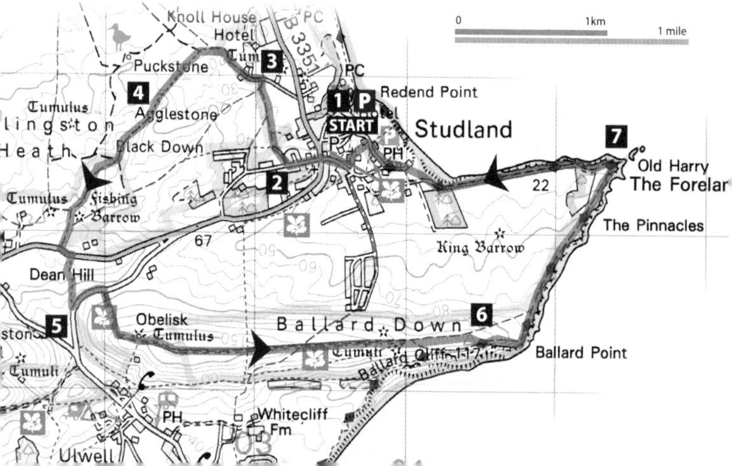

Seaside rock?: *The 400-tonne Agglestone, or 'Holy stone', perches on Godlingston Heath*

3. Meeting a broad gravel track, follow it left and continue beyond its end along a wooded path onto **Godlingston Heath**. Over a **footbridge** beside a ford, turn left towards a large rock ahead, bearing left again where the path shortly forks. Breaking from the trees, your objective soon appears across the heath. Keep left at the next fork and head for the massive **Agglestone**.

Jutting out into Poole Bay, Studland Foreland guards the entrance to Poole Harbour and the ancient Saxon stronghold of Wareham. But the place was important long before then, evidenced by the find of an Iron Age logboat in the bogs of what is now Wareham Forest and artefacts showing a trade in jewellery, iron and stone goods across the water with France.

4. Keep going beyond the rock, eventually crossing a junction of paths to pass through consecutive gates. Meeting a broader trail, go right and later keep right at a fork. Ignoring golfers' paths, carry on, crossing the fairway on the **Isle of Purbeck golf course**

Pale beauty: *Old Harry's chalk arches and stacks were once connected to Ballard Down*

to come out onto the **Studland road**. Cross the road and go briefly left to a stile on the right. Strike out across another segment of the golf course to find a yellow post marking a path into the trees opposite. Drop left to a stile and then bear right across bracken and rough meadow to emerge over a final stile onto another road.

5. Turn left along the verge, crossing after 300 metres to leave on a path through a gate that climbs straight ahead onto **Ballard Down**. Curving left, continue past an **obelisk** and on along the broad ridge, from which views open either side to Swanage and Poole, and eventually ahead to the Isle of Wight.

Ballard's obelisk was originally erected in 1892 by George Burt (see Durlston Head) to celebrate the provision of a municipal water supply to Swanage. During the Second World War, it was dismantled to prevent Luftwaffe pilots using it as a landmark during their raids along the south coast. It was finally rebuilt in 1973 by the soldiers of the Territorials.

6. Towards the far end, passing a **trig column**, bear right to a gate and walk on to join the **coast path**. Continue

around **Ballard Point** and gently down to **Handfast Point**, off which are the famous **Pinnacles** and **Old Harry Rocks**.

7. Swinging around the headland, the path steps back from the cliffs behind trees, eventually joining a tarmac drive. Follow it left to a lane by **toilets** and go right past the **Bankes Arms** back to the car park to complete the walk. ♦

Agglestone Rock

The massive Agglestone ironstone boulder once balanced on a pedestal, rearing from the heathery landscape like a giant flat-topped anvil. Erosion of the softer rock at its base eventually left it unbalanced and sometime in the mid-20th century, it toppled over. Geologists suggest it may be a remnant left by natural weathering or even quarrying, but legend says it was hurled from the Isle of Wight by a giant trying to raze Corfe Castle.

Useful Information

Visit Dorset

Dorset's official tourism website covers everything from accommodation and special events to attractions and adventure. **www.visit-dorset.com**

Jurassic Coast World Heritage Site

The Jurassic Coast website also has background information on geology and fossils as well as a host of practical details to help plan your visit. **www.jurassiccoast.org**

Tourist Information Centres

The main TICs provide free information on everything from accommodation and transport to what's on and walking advice.

Bournemouth TIC	01202 451734	www.bournemouth.co.uk
Bridport TIC	01308 424901	www.visit-dorset.com
Dorchester TIC	01305 267992	www.visit-dorset.com
Lyme Regis TIC	01297 442138	www.visit-dorset.com
Poole TIC	01202 262600	www.pooletourism.com
Swanage TIC	01929 422885	www.visitswanageandpurbeck.co.uk
Discover Purbeck TIC	01929 552740	www.visitswanageandpurbeck.co.uk
Weymouth TIC	01305 783225	www.visitweymouth.co.uk

Weather

Online weather forecasts for Dorset are available from the Met Office at: **www.metoffice.gov.uk**

Rail Travel

Main railway stations are located at Bournemouth, Dorchester Poole, Wareham, and Weymouth. Information is available from National Rail Enquiries on 08457 484950 or **www.nationalrail.com.uk** There is also a heritage rail service between Wareham and Swanage; 01929 425800 or **www.swanagerailway.co.uk**

Bus Travel

Many places along the Dorset coast are served by bus. Information is available from Travel Dorset **www.dorsetforyou.gov.uk** or traveline **www.travelinesw.com**

Camping

Dorset is a popular area for camping, with many sites owned by or affiliated to the Camping and Caravanning Club; 024 7647 5426 | **www.campingandcaravanningclub.co.uk**